Extremist Islamic Terrorist Organizations: Dangers for the Present and Future

Thomas W. Allen

AIR COMMAND AND STAFF COLLEGE

AIR UNIVERSITY

Extremist Islamic Terrorist Organizations: Dangers for the Present and Future

by

Thomas W. Allen, Major, USAF

A Research Report Submitted to the Faculty

In Partial Fulfillment of the Graduation Requirements

Advisor: Dr Lewis K. Griffith

Maxwell Air Force Base, Alabama

April 2008

Distribution A: Approved for Public Release; distribution unlimited

AU/ACSC/ALLENT/AY08

Disclaimer

The views expressed in this academic research paper are those of the author(s) and do not reflect the official policy or position of the US government or the Department of Defense. In accordance with Air Force Instruction 51-303, it is not copyrighted, but is the property of the United States government.

AU/ACSC/ALLENT/AY08

Contents

Page

DISCLAIMER ii

PREFACE iv

ABSTRACT v

CHAPTER 1 – INTRODUCTION 1
    Overview 1

CHAPTER 2 – EXTREMIST ISLAMIC TERRORIST ORGANIZATIONS 3
    The Muslim Brotherhood 3
    Al Qaeda 6
    A Direct Correlation 10

CHAPTER 3 – LITERATURE REVIEW AND FINDINGS 12
    Research Methodology 12
    Research Challenges 12
    Literature Review 13
    What are EITOs Attempting to Achieve by Recruiting New Members? 14
    Why are EITOs Recruiting New Members? 14
    How are EITOs Recruiting New Members? 15
    Where are EITOs Recruiting New Members? 16
    Who are EITOs Recruiting? 18
    When are EITOs Recruiting New Members? 19
    A Concern for the Future 20

CHAPTER 4 – FUTURE CONCERNS 22

CHAPTER 5 – CONCLUSIONS AND RECOMMENDATIONS 26
    Recommendations 27

END NOTES 29

BIBLIOGRAPHY 32

AU/ACSC/ALLENT/AY08

Preface

On September 11th 2001 the attack on the Pentagon literally shook my family as they were enjoying their morning together in Alexandria, Virginia. Within hours, I left the Joint Military Intelligence College, only to sit in D.C. traffic for hours smelling the smoke streaming from the Pentagon and listening to reports of the Twin Towers collapsing. I felt particularly worthless the remainder of that year, as I completed school and Al Qaeda planned future attacks. However, a deep personal interest in counter-terrorism was born, and this paper is a result of that experience.

The United States has been fighting the Global War on Terrorism for over 7 years and while progress has been made, the threat of future attacks by Extremist Islamic Terrorist Organizations (EITO) remains. During my War on Terrorism class this year, a reading on terrorist recruiting methods captured my attention and this paper is the result of my research efforts. I believe that the only way to defeat EITOs will be by fully understanding their ideological goals and recruiting methodologies and stopping extremist Muslims from joining EITOs. I hope the research I conducted and the recommendations provided are used by appropriate counter-terrorism organizations for further analysis and examination. If this analysis can help the United States further focus its counter-terrorism efforts, to prevent another 9/11 from ever occurring on American soil again, it was worth every minute spent conducting research and writing it.

I want to offer my deepest appreciation to my wife Tisha for all her support while I was conducting research and writing this paper. I am deeply grateful to Dr Griffith for his advice, guidance, and encouragement. A special thanks to the entire Fairchild Library staff, who answered countless questions and helped acquire over a dozen books for me from libraries throughout the United States. Finally, a deep hearted thank you to Ashley and Manny for their support and understanding why they had to be quiet while their Dad was in "time-out," yet again.

AU/ACSC/ALLENT/AY08

Abstract

United States (US) counter-terrorism efforts to date have been reactionary in nature and occur after terrorists have been recruited and trained. To develop an adequate counter-terrorism program, the US must focus its efforts at the onset of any Extremist Islamic Terrorist Organizations (EITO) planning stages. Optimally, this means preventing Muslims from joining EITOs. To accomplish this analysts need to fully understand EITOs ideological goals, which in turn explains what EITOs are attempting to achieve when recruiting as well as why, how, where, and who they are recruiting. Analysis reveals EITOs recruit new members, to achieve their objectives and they are using active and passive recruiting techniques, 24 hours a day, 365 days out of the year. They also attempt to recruit men and women, as long as they are Muslims, as support personnel and operators who can conduct attacks. EITO recruitment is conducted world-wide, in both physical and virtual locations. If analysts better understand these recruiting methodologies they will be able to develop tactics, techniques, and procedures to neutralize their recruiting methodologies and defeat EITOs before they conduct another attack. If analysts fail to defeat EITO recruiting methodologies, an EITO, specifically AQ, will be able to recruit non-traditional Muslims to infiltrate and conduct attacks within the US.

AU/ACSC/ALLENT/AY08

Chapter 1 – Introduction

Al Qaeda (AQ), an Extremist Islamic Terrorist Organization (EITO), conducted a series of then unimaginable terrorist attacks on September 11th 2001 when a small number of terrorists managed to hijack three commercial airplanes, turn them into guided weapons, and kill 3,025 people…all without the benefit of any non-traditional Muslim recruits.[1] Usama bin Laden stated both before and after the attacks of 9/11 that he wanted to attack the United States (US) directly as he continues his "jihad" against the West. Thus, future attacks within the US are a near certainty unless the US can identify and prevent these attacks. However, US counter-terrorism efforts to date have been reactionary in nature and attempts to minimize attacks occur only after terrorists have been recruited, organized, and trained.

To develop an adequate counter-terrorism program, the US must make a concerted effort to interdict terrorist organizations at the onset of their planning stages. Optimally, this means preventing potential recruits from joining EITOs. To accomplish this there are several questions which have not been addressed adequately to date: Why are EITOs recruiting new members? Who are EITOs recruiting? When and where are EITOs recruiting new members? How are EITOs recruiting new members? And finally, what are EITOs achieving by recruiting new members? If counter-terrorism analysts answer these questions they will be able to develop better tactics, techniques, and procedures to neutralize EITO efforts to recruit new members and possibly prevent future attacks within the US and eventually defeat the EITOs.

Overview

Before an analyst can hope to understand the recruiting methodologies being employed by EITOs they must understand who they are fighting. The State Department's "Country Reports on Terrorism 2006" officially identifies 23 Extremist Islamic or Muslim terrorist organizations, which are extracted from the Department of Treasury's Specially Designated Nationals list.[2] However, while conducting research for this paper, sources indicate there are at least 50 EITOs in existence. To understand the history and ideological goals of every one of these EITOs is beyond the scope of this paper. However, an examination of the history, leadership, and ideological goals of the first EITO, the Muslim Brotherhood (MB) as well as AQ, currently the most active and violent EITO, is critical in establishing a basic understanding of the ideological goals of EITOs. This understanding provides the foundation for this paper and also helped focus research efforts to identify EITO recruiting methodologies. Findings are presented in Chapter 2. Chapter 3 identifies the research methodology used to identify sources for this paper and discusses difficulties faced while conducting research. It then details what, why, how, where, who, and when EITOs are recruiting new members. Chapter 4 presents a daunting future concern for US counter-terrorism officials based on numerous findings in the research material indicating an EITO, specifically AQ, is recruiting non-traditional Muslims to infiltrate, support, and conduct attacks against the US. Chapter 5 summarizes the findings of this paper and then presents several recommended areas for further analysis as well as a strategy for neutralizing EITO recruiting efforts.

Research for this paper included a detailed examination of available books, government publications, research papers, newspapers, journals, web-pages, academic publications, and professional reports, from both the US, and foreign countries. Additionally, only unclassified sources were used. Therefore, this paper is intended to be used as a basis for further analysis by appropriate local, state, and national counter-terrorism organizations, using all source intelligence, regardless of classification level.

Chapter 2 – Extremist Islamic Terrorist Organizations

Before any analyst can hope to determine how the enemy operates, let alone defeat it, they must comprehend; who the enemy is, where they originated from, and what constitutes the core and political levels of its cultural pyramid. There are over 50 EITOs operating around the world, however, two are by far the most well known and studied; the MB and AQ.[3] Because the MB has had both direct and indirect influences on many modern EITOs, especially AQ, understanding both their leaders and why they were established will provide a clearer understanding of how EITOs operates and focus further analysis efforts to develop counter-measures to neutralize their recruiting efforts.

The Muslim Brotherhood

Hassan al Banna is considered to be the founding father of the MB, serving as its charismatic and visionary leader from 1928 to 1948. Al Banna grew up in an Egypt under English rule. During this time, especially in the late 1920's, England regularly exploited local Egyptian citizens, particularly during the construction of the Suez Canal, while simultaneously failing to remain sensitive to local Islamic customs and beliefs.[4] Furthermore, al Banna was educated and raised by his father, the town's charismatic Islamic leader, who also ruled over his family based on traditional conservative or Hanbali Islamic beliefs. After his initial education under his father's tutelage, al Banna attended secondary school. This began his gradual radicalization process where he became a member of the Society for Islamic Morality. Here he became responsible for ensuring his peers followed strict Muslim behavior codes.[5] Upon completing secondary school al Banna attended college and was exposed to liberal Muslim views for the first time. Many of al Banna's classmates practiced Sufi Islam and demonstrated a greater tolerance for western ideas and values, which caused al Banna to seek fellow conservative Muslims while completing college. Shortly after completing college, al Banna became a school teacher and subsequently moved near Cairo, Egypt.[6]

It was at this time al Banna was fully exposed to the influence of Western "decadence" and more liberal style of living displayed in the city. After being taken aback by this disregard for Muslim principles, al Banna founded the Ikwan Al Muslimun, or what is known today as the MB in 1928.[7] In establishing the MB, al Banna hoped to peacefully reemphasize the political orientation of Islam, thus reforming the Government of Egypt to adhere to the "true" Quranic principles. Al Banna was not alone in his sentiment to see Egypt ruled by Islamic law, but at that time MB called only for political, not violent, action. It was not until al Banna was sent to prison in 1941 that the MB turned violent.[8]

After being sent to prison al Banna became more committed to activism and he helped found a violent off-shoot of the MB to bring political changes.[9] In their first major act of violence the MB joined fellow Arabs in Palestine during the 1948 Arab Israeli War. This action increased the MB's credibility amongst Middle Eastern Muslims and served as a recruiting tool. In 1948 the MB was officially banished by Egyptian Prime Minister al-Nuqrashi.[10] The MB responded to this declaration by assassinating al-Nugrashi and al Banna was subsequently executed by Egyptian police two months later. Shortly thereafter, Egyptian President Gamal Abdel Nasser sent many MB members to prison, which pressured the MB to go underground.

During this same period a new charismatic, and vehemently anti-western, member of the MB rose to prominence, Sayyid Qutb. Qutb was directly exposed to, and utterly appalled at, the decadence of western values, when he lived in the US for a short period of time. Upon returning to Egypt he wrote "Guideposts" which established the foundations for modern militant Islam and the strict Saudi version of Islam known as Wahhabism was brought into MB ideology.[11] Many historians believe that while al Banna was the founder of the MB, Qutb was actually the most intellectual leader and it was his influential writings and thoughts that started the MB's radical anti-western stance. Qutb published his most influential book "Milestones" in 1964 which essentially declared it was the duty of every true Muslim to spread Islam by whatever means available including the use of violence if necessary. Thus, the radicalization of the MB accelerated and their influence spread to over 70 nations, including the US. In 1966 Qutb, like al Banna was executed. The executions of both men served to solidify their positions as martyrs, ensuring that their messages would serve as motivators for future terrorists.

Throughout the MB's history it has made an effort to recruit from a wide swath of the Muslim populous, relying on its extremist and radicalized ideology. Their efforts to recruit new members can be traced to the very prisons that held al Banna, to universities, mosques, and sports clubs. In fact several publications indicate that the MB was willing to accept any Muslim as a member as long as they accepted the principles of the organization. This explains the rapid growth and success the MB had amassing an estimated 500,000 to 2,000,000 members (actual numbers vary depending on source used) world-wide.[12] Current MB membership numbers are not fully known as the group has become more secretive since 1954 and the failed assassination attempt of then Egyptian President Nasser. The MB continues to operation internationally, however, its existence remains veiled in secrecy as they recruit, gain funding, and support under various pseudo-named organizations. While the MB's ability to recruit members around the world poses a potential threat to the US, the greater threat is the impact the MB has had on EITOs which threaten US interests, specifically, AQ.

Al Qaeda

If al Banna is the founding father of the MB, then Usama bin Laden should be considered the founding father of AQ. To fully understand what made bin Laden into the charismatic leader of AQ, analysts must understand not only who the major influences were in his life, but also key events of his life. Bin Laden was raised by his family in the Wahabite traditions.[13] Thus, bin Laden, much like al Banna, began his life following in his father's footsteps as a devout conservative Muslim. However, while al Banna's father influenced his faith, bin Laden's father, Mohammed bin Laden, also influenced his work ethic and even fanaticism. Bin Laden's father was originally raised in Yemen as a simple peasant and porter, but immigrated to Saudi Arabia in the 1920s and established what would eventually become an international construction company. Bin Laden was influenced not only by his father's business "know how," but his devotion to Islam, generous and humble nature, and personality. John F. Burns, writer for the New York Times, goes so far to say, "Those around here [in Yemen] who knew his father say the key to bin Laden's character -- his shrewdness and singularity of purpose, his deeply conservative religious and political views, his profound distaste for non-Islamic influences that have penetrated some of the most remote corners of old Arabia, even the cunning tradecraft he has used in his meticulously planned attacks."[14] Although the death of his father did not constitute a turning point in bin Laden's life, this event must be considered in context since he lost the most influential and calming person in his life at a young age. Bin Laden's inheritance, estimated at over $300 million US dollars, however, has helped finance many of AQ's operations.

Prior to his father's death, the Bin Laden's were held in very high esteem throughout the Middle East in the 1960's and 1970's. Mohammed bin Laden, after working on King Saud's palace renovations, so impressed King Saud with his capabilities, that he awarded construction contracts to renovate two of the holiest Mosques in Mecca and Medina respectively.[15] Because of the high visibility of these projects, the bin Ladens began building personal relationships with leading Islamic leaders throughout the Middle East who traveled to Mecca during their yearly pilgrimages. Usama bin Laden's direct access to these two Mosques also had an indirect effect as reports indicate he had his first interactions with the MB and radical Islam at this time.[16]

Bin Laden became even more radical in his beliefs while attending King Abul Aziz University via the writings of fundamentalist Islamic scholars. The most influential of these scholars was the MB's Sayyid Qutb.[17] As discussed earlier, Qutb's writings were the impetus behind the MB's movement to a more militant organization. Thus, the seeds of discontent and extremism were being sewn into bin Laden's subconscious. All he needed now was a spark to ignite the fire within to establish his own radical Islamic organization and wage a "jihad" against non-believers world-wide. This flash point occurred when he organized, personally funded, and later joined the Mujahedin in the battle for Afghanistan in the 1980's.

Shortly after the 1979 Soviet invasion of Afghanistan bin Laden began making trips to Pakistan to determine what equipment the Mujahedin needed as well as transporting funds from several Gulf nations to pay for the war. Bin Laden's role soon changed from that of a supplier and financier to an active participant in the battle for sovereignty against a non-Islamic state. This metamorphosis is strikingly similar to the change al Banna undertook while imprisoned during England's rule of Egypt. Bin Laden's trips into Pakistan continued until 1982 when he began moving some of the bin Laden family's construction equipment into Afghanistan. Bin Laden also used his construction expertise as a "contractor to the "jihad"" to build tunnels and shelters in the mountains of Afghanistan for use by Mujahedin fighters.[18] His involvement in Afghanistan deepened in 1984 when he established the predecessor to AQ, the Maktabu L-Khidama (MAK).

MAK was established in 1984 by bin Laden in conjunction with Abdallah Azzam, a leader of the Palestinian MB, to recruit young Muslims to fight against the Soviets.[19] MAK was actually only one of seven organizations established to move international funding, equipment, and Muslim fighters into Afghanistan. Ironically, because of the ongoing Cold War between the US and Soviet Union the Central Intelligence Agency and Pakistani Inter-Services Intelligence Agency indirectly supplied arms and funding to MAK to continue the war.[20] MAK also represents the most direct connection between bin Laden, AQ, and the MB to date. The fact that bin Laden and Azzam worked together to recruit new MAK members provides reasonable evidence that some of the MB and AQ's recruitment methods and means may be similar.

While the MAK successfully recruited new members, Azzam and bin Laden realized the Islamic movement needed to grow on a grander scale and AQ was established prior to the end of the war for this very purpose. However, both men believed the movement needed to move in different directions. Azzam did not want AQ to become a terrorist organization and believed any violence against fellow Muslims violated Islamic law. In stark contrast, bin Laden wanted to use AQ as a central organization to wage a violent "jihad" against Egypt and other secular Muslim regimes.[21] Thus, the two men went in separate directions and bin Laden became the leader of AQ. What made him the right man at the time was three fold: First, his success as the leader of the MAK and Mujahedin gave instant credibility to AQ. Second, his charismatic personality and contacts with Mujahedin fighters gave him ready access to combat trained recruits. Finally, his previous recruiting efforts with the MAK gave AQ unparalleled access to many states around the world. Thus, the stage was set for AQ to become, a world-wide networked organization fighting a "jihad" against non-believers. However, events in the 1990's gave bin Laden a true enemy to focus AQ's efforts against and brought him in contact with yet another MB member.

After the Afghanistan war, bin Laden returned to Saudi Arabia as a hero. However, this status changed overnight in 1990 after Iraq invaded Kuwait. When Iraq was poised at the Saudi border and an invasion appeared imminent, bin Laden offered to defend Saudi Arabia with his Mujahedin forces. Instead the Royal family allowed a US led coalition into Saudi Arabia to defend the country, and in doing so insulted bin Laden, AQ, and his fellow Mujahedin. Adding to bin Laden's growing hatred of the US and the Royal family was the permanent basing of US troops in Saudi Arabia following the Gulf War. These events contributed to his vocal criticisms of the Saudi Royal family, declaration of a defensive "jihad," and ultimately his banishment to Sudan in 1991.[22] During this same period Dr. Ayman al Zawahiri, a known Islamic extremist and member of the MB, became bin Laden's second in command and began to define the ideological strategy for AQ's ongoing violent and offensive "jihad" against the US and other Muslim nations whose countries were ruled by secular law. The importance of al Zawahiri cannot be understated as it is he, not bin Laden, who produced publications explaining the ideological goals of AQ based on the writings of al Banna and Qutb.

While commonalities in the history and leaders of AQ and the MB are abundant, their ideological goals are also remarkably similar. AQ's goals and ideology have been gradually changed over the last 28 years by both bin Laden and al Zawahiri, to recruit new members as well as maintain support for their "jihad." The primary goal of AQ is to drive US influence from the Middle East in a "greater jihad,"[23] while simultaneously overthrowing illegitimate regimes in the region in pursuit of "true Islam,"[24] establishment of one global…Caliphite and "Genuine" Muslim state in the heart of the Arab world,[25] destroying Israel,[26] and finally expanding the "jihad" into non-Arab Islamic countries to rally and strengthen a global "jihad."[27] In January 2005, al Zawahiri identified "three foundations" to clarify AQ's ideological goals to include; the liberation of all Muslim lands of any western presence, the establishment of Quran-based authority to govern in all Islamic states based on Sharia law, and the liberation of human beings to enable Muslims to overthrow rulers who violate Islamic laws and principles.[28] Ironically, in al Zawahiri's "Three Foundations" he professes that AQ and every Muslim should accomplish these goals by using any means possible, even if they run contrary to Islamic law.[29]

The MB movement web-page identifies six MB objectives to include; building the Muslim individual, family, society, state, and Khiafa or unity between the Islamic states, and finally, mastering the world with Islam.[30] To achieve these objectives the MB professes a five-part theme. It is with this theme that the ideological goals of AQ roughly correlate with the MB. It includes: 1.) Allah is our objective, 2.) the messenger (Allah) is our leader, 3.) the Quran is our law, 4.) "jihad" is our way, 5.) dying in the way of Allah is our highest hope.[31]

A Direct Correlation

Based on the previous examination of the MB's and AQ's histories, several commonalities between the organizations and their leaders are evident. While there are slight variations between the ideological goals of AQ and the objectives of the MB many similarities exist. The fact that bin Laden studied the works of the MB from an early age and then founded both the MAK and AQ with the assistance of influential MB members cannot be refuted. Additionally, the presence of al Zawahiri, a former MB member, as AQ's strategist and bin Laden's number two man, cements the commonalities between the two organizations.

The linkages between the MB and bin Laden/AQ also make it highly likely that the recruiting methodologies employed by both organizations are also similar. Based on the world-wide influence and presence of the MB and the linkages between AQ and many of the EITOs identified in the State Department's "Country Reports on Terrorism 2006" it is not unreasonable to postulate that any recruiting methodologies used by these two organizations are simultaneously being used by other EITOs such as the Abu Sayyaf Group, Al-Aqsa Martyrs Brigade, Al-Jihad, Ansar al-Islam, Armed Islamic Group, Jemaah Islamiyah, and the Moro Islamic Liberation Front to name but a few.

Chapter 3 – Literature Review and Findings

Research Methodology

When conducting research, analysts must have a clear objective of what they are hoping to prove. To focus their research efforts, analysts are also taught to question the source of their information. Thus, of the 900 plus sources and web-sites accesses, the attached Bibliography identifies only sources which contained accurate academic level information warranting inclusion in this paper. Analysts are also taught to use the 5W's (and a H) as a litmus test to determine if they have a comprehensive understanding of the enemies intentions. Therefore, these six questions were used to attempt to determine; what are EITOs attempting to achieve when recruiting new members as well as why, how, where, who, and when EITOs are recruiting new members.

Research Challenges

The biggest challenge faced while gathering sources for this paper was sorting through the wealth of information available on the internet. The reliability and originating authors for dozens of documents could not be confirmed, thus making many of the publications useless. Additionally, numerous publications, such as the <u>Al Qaeda Training Manual</u> and <u>Al Qaeda: Casting a Shadow of Terror</u> have been re-printed under different names due to the ongoing interest in EITOs, especially AQ. Further complicating research efforts were the overabundance of available information via the numerous unofficial publications posted on web-pages by self proclaimed "experts." These web-pages ran the gamut from 9/11 conspiracy theorists and white supremacy groups to self proclaimed "jihad Watch Groups." On many occasions however, these sites referenced or posted references that were later located, evaluated, and used by the author regardless of the web-site owner's agenda. Such was the case when several questionable sources cited James Forest as a terrorism expert. Additional research confirmed the identity and credentials of James J. F. Forest, Director of Terrorism Studies at the US Military Academy. Subsequently, several of Forest's publications were instrumental in the writing this paper.

Literature Review

A detailed examination of over 160 sources revealed EITOs are conducting multifaceted recruiting efforts. Not surprisingly, AQ was by far the most mentioned and examined EITO due to the violent nature of recent attacks as well attacks thwarted by law enforcement agencies around the world. The MB was the second most written about EITO due to the global presence of their organization. However, of the remaining 45 plus EITOs only the Jemaah Islamiyah, and Abu Sayyaf Group were mentioned periodically.

Sources attempting to identify who EITOs are recruiting constituted the bulk of available material used to compose this paper as this aspect of terrorism appears to have garnered the most research interest to date. Very few sources directly addressed what EITOs are attempting to achieve by recruiting new members. Instead this information had to be extracted from the limited number of sources which identified why terrorist organizations are recruiting new members. Sources did indicate that recruits are needed to replace members who die as well as to plan and organize future attacks while helping EITOs expand and achieve their goals. Not one source identified when EITOs recruit new members.

Multiple Sources did identify where and how EITO's are recruiting. The internet, mosques, and prisons are the three most prolific recruiting locations and means being used. The Internet was the most widely written about recruiting medium and is also used as a communication medium which has a global reach and also affords EITOs with some operational security from counter-terrorism efforts. Conversely, only a few sources specifically identified why EITOs recruit new members. Again, this question seems to be taken as an assumption by various authors. The bottom line is EITOs recruit new members to expand their influence, replace members killed while conducting attacks, and support operations. The remainder of this chapter will synthesize and detail EITO recruiting methodologies.

What are EITOs Attempting to Achieve by Recruiting New Members?

EITOs need to recruit new member to achieve their goal and objectives. For example, AQ needs new recruits to achieve their "three foundations" to include; the liberation of all Muslim lands of any western presence, the establishment of Quran-based authority to govern in all Islamic states based on Sharia law, and the liberation of human beings to enable Muslims to overthrow rulers who violate Islamic laws and principles.[32] Thus, to fully understand why every EITO recruits new members each of their ideological goals must be understood. By understanding the ideological goals of EITOs the context of remaining 5 pieces of the analytical puzzle can be put into proper context to conduct further analysis. Additionally, as Cindy Combs suggests, "In order to recruit effectively, groups must convey a clear sense of purpose and identity to those who might be seeking similar political goals."[33] Thus, while it is critical for EITOs to have a clear sense of purpose to recruit effectively; it is equally import in understanding what EITO recruiting methodologies are to counter them.

Why are EITOs Recruiting New Members?

Every EITO, including AQ, must recruit new members to "replace losses, acquire new talent, and expand their reach...fill the slots left by those who have been "martyred" in attacks or captured by counter-terrorism forces."[34] Thus, EITOs are like any military organization or business and must have people who conduct a myriad of tasks and these tasks change over time. Subsequently, recruiting efforts by EITOs are designed to attract support personnel as well as militant members who will conduct attacks, depending on the organizations method of achieving their goals and objectives. Numerous references indicate the MB's recruitment requirements reflected similar needs over the last 70 plus years. The bottom line is EITOs need recruits who they can train to work in every aspect of the terrorist planning and execution cycle to include; fundraising, scouting, intelligence, recruiting, leadership, technology, and logistics to name but a few and are very much like a military organization. The Al Qaeda Training Manual was the only EITO document that identified key personnel and missions that an EITO needs to develop an effective terrorist organization.[35]

How are EITOs Recruiting New Members?

Knowing why EITOs need to recruit new members only scratches the surface when attempting to understand the remaining pieces of the analytical puzzle. Thus, a detailed understanding of how EITOs conduct recruiting is needed. EITOs, in particular AQ and the MB recruit in two unique manners. Specifically, these two EITO's actively attempt to contact potential recruits and get them to join, much like military recruiters. However, they also use passive recruiting techniques to slowly develop extremist mentalities in vulnerable people and encourage them to contact their organizations. It is important to understand that these two EITO methodologies can occur simultaneously regardless of the medium used.[36]

The Internet and media serve as both active and passive recruiting methods. Both communication forms serve a myriad of purposes to include; legitimization, mobilization, networking, propaganda, recruitment, indoctrination, and fundraising. The internet allows EITOs to focus their recruiting efforts at a specific target audience while protecting itself from counter-terrorism experts through the use of password protected web-sites.[37] The internet also allows EITOs to post a myriad of material espousing its ideology which appeals to a widely varied audience of potential recruits every minute of every day. Unique recruiting materials previously used include; extremist music and rap videos, interviews with EITO leaders, and free role playing games where potential recruits play as "jihadist's" fighting US forces.[38] This type of passive and seemingly sublime recruiting is then used to get people to become a member of an EITO like AQ.

The Internet has opened new avenues for terrorist organizations to exploit. Specifically, as Marc Sageman suggest, "The internet can be used to [passively] attract isolated individuals by bringing them together with others who share their frustrations and despair and identifies them to recruiters who can [actively] put them in touch with other recruiters or propaganda used to make their views even more extreme."[39] In turn, the use of the Internet provides EITOs with security measures as potential recruits can be pre-screened before they are approached. While the internet initially appeared to be the primary avenue for recruitment, analysis has revealed EITOs are conducting recruitment activities in a variety of locales around the world.

Where are EITOs Recruiting New Members?

EITOs recruit new members on nearly every continent in the world. This includes physical as well as on-line virtual meeting locations. Thus, many EITOs appear to follow the MB's proven methodology of recruiting in as many states as possible while taking the time to individualize their efforts depending on the situation and audience. EITOs also appear to recruit in multiple locations to include; prisons, mosques, universities, informal meeting locations, and as mentioned previously, the Internet. With the exception of the Internet, these locations put potential recruits in a controlled location where EITOs can evaluate their commitment while simultaneously pushing their own recruiting pitch. The extent of EITO and especially AQ's recruiting efforts is daunting as described by Jessica Stern, "Al Qaeda operatives appear to have been recruited in their home countries throughout the Middle East. However several countries have uncovered AQ linked Islamic organizations within their own borders to include Spain, Italy, Belgium, Germany, Pakistan, Indonesia, and Malaysia"[40] While the US is not specifically mentioned, the presence of the MB, extremist mosques, and the identification of several US citizens as EITO and AQ members indicate recruiting is occurring within the US.

Inmates are prime recruiting candidates for EITOs as the have already committed violent crimes and have little to no loyalty to their nations and are also being isolated from their families and friends.[41] Proof of this vulnerability resides in the successful recruiting of Jose Padilla and Richard Reid, two known AQ members.[42] Prisons are fertile EITO recruiting grounds as many prisoners seek to find their faith after being incarcerated and some prison Chaplains are in turn preaching radicalized versions of Islam to those seeking faith. Numerous reports indicate prison Chaplains teach converts about the spiritual benefits of becoming a Muslim while simultaneously professing how and why the system has failed the inmate and that it is the state which is ultimately responsible for their actions as a method of disassociation. Statistics indicate that up to 15-20% of prison inmates are recruited and converted to Islam.[43] Counter-terrorism efforts in prisons have been complicated as trends are extremely difficult to identify because not all prison systems are interlinked. Additionally, this is a problem which EITOs exploit as prison Chaplains teach traditional Wahhabi-based Islam, which corresponds with most EITO ideological goals.[44]

Mosques continue to serve as a key EITO recruiting location. Quintan Wiktorowicz best summarizes the importance of the mosque to Islam when he writes, "The multi-functionality of the mosque, its communal dimensions, and its centrality in neighborhoods not only serve the needs of the community, but also create a potential institution for revolutionary action."[45] Thus, while the mosque serves the spiritual and communal needs of devout Muslims it simultaneously serves as an EITO recruiting location. Mosques remain difficult to monitor as law enforcement and government agencies cannot prevent people from practicing their religion in most states around the world. Sources continue to indicate that mosque's remain critical to EITO recruiting methodologies as they are used as vetting tools to assess a recruit's commitment. EITOs then physically contact recruits outside of mosques in universities, gyms, or social clubs.[46]

Universities are a focal point for EITO recruiting as it generates a pool of economically and socially diverse recruits in both the US and EU/UK. The UK produced Whitehall dossier found, "Extremists are known to target schools and colleges where young people may be very inquisitive but less challenging and more susceptible to extremist reasoning/arguments."[47] Similarly, Islamic centers and organizations like the American Muslim Council and the Islamic Society of North America are used as support mechanisms for many Islamic immigrants who suffer from feelings of alienation and prejudice in their new states. EITOs then use these vulnerabilities to gradually present their ideologies, and then recruit them at their most vulnerable moment. While the first four analytical puzzle pieces have been answered, the question of who are EITOs recruiting remains unanswered.

Who are EITOS Recruiting?

Perhaps the most vexing question facing counter-terrorism analysts is who is a potential recruit. According to the Al Qaeda Training Manual the primary requirement to become a member of their EITO is that a recruit must be Muslim, but ethnicity does not matter.[48] Other than requiring new members to be a Muslim EITOs appear to recruit anyone who indicates they have an interest in joining their organization regardless of education or experience levels. Not one source identified any other requirements. It appears that EITOs evaluate new recruits during training conducted within their own organization or at external training camps and then put new members in specific jobs taking advantage of their abilities while mitigating shortfalls in their education or physical abilities. Thus, new recruits who demonstrate physical and situational awareness skills may be put into attack cells, where as a new recruit who is small in stature but well educated and computer literate may be identified and assigned to a technology or recruiting cell.

The most valuable recruits to an EITO are recent converts to Islam who self recruit and actively seek out EITO members. This normally occurs without the assistance of EITO recruiters and does not necessarily involve the mosque.[49] Self recruits also complicate counter recruiting efforts as they are extremely difficult to profile. The inherent difficulties of identifying who potential recruits may be is evident in the number of sources which repeatedly indicated that recruits come from varied backgrounds and are not just the poor or uneducated nor are they only from failing or failed states. Furthermore, Daniel Pipes, director of The Middle East Forum, suggests "[M]ilitant Islam attracts highly competent, motivated, and ambitious individuals…far from the laggards of society."[50] In fact, a large number of EITO recruits are university students who are attracted to extremist Islamic messages being pitched on campuses. This suggests EITO passive recruiting techniques are enabling young Muslims, who want to join EITOs but don't know how, to use contact information on the internet, in videos, or in computer games to identify themselves to that organization. While knowing who EITOs are trying to recruit is important, analysts also need to know when EITOs are recruiting new members.

When are EITOs Recruiting New Members?

As mentioned earlier in this chapter, available literature did not directly address this piece of the analytical puzzle. Thus, the following findings are suppositions based on available information and the author's 13 years of experience as an Intelligence Officer in the US Air

Force. Based on EITO tendencies to use many of the MB's recruiting methodologies both active and passive, as well as their own, it is assessed that they recruit new members 24 hours a day, 7 days a week, 365 days out of the year. EITOs are able to do this because of their combined use of passive and active recruiting methodologies. By establishing and making passive recruiting material available to potential recruits, specifically through the internet, not unlike all four branches of the US military, EITO messages and recruiting pitches are omni-present.

Additionally, EITOs are also able to reach many potential recruits via the media whenever it makes typed or recorded messages from their leaders available. The media then broadcasts these messages world-wide. AQ's often released verbal and visual video tapes of messages fro bin Laden and al Zawahiri are prime examples of this type of recruiting material. Similarly, any coverage of an EITO's attack provides their organization and cause with free publicity.

Finally, as discussed earlier, EITOs are using active and passive recruiting techniques, 24 hours a day, to simultaneously attract men and women who not only self recruit but also sympathize with extremist Islamic messages from prisons and local mosques to universities, sports clubs, and informal meeting locations. EITOs then use various methodologies to further these individual's thoughts and beliefs until they become actual recruits.

A Concern for the Future

While conducting research for this paper a recurring theme kept appearing in various sources that immediately grabbed the author's attention. It appears that while the recruiting methodologies of terrorists are multifaceted, omnipresent, and must be countered to defeat EITOs, there is a greater future concern for the US. It appears AQ is purposefully recruiting men and women who do not match the typical Muslim male counter-terrorism profile and have valid

US or EU passports allowing AQ access into western states. If AQ successfully recruits new members with these credentials it will be much easier for them to avoid counter-terrorism efforts and conduct future attacks within the US. This future threat is detailed in Chapter 4.

Chapter 4 – Future Concerns

While conducting research for this paper a potential threat to the US became evident that may not be fully understood by counter-terrorism analysts. It appears AQ is purposefully attempting to recruit non-traditional Muslims who can gain legitimate and unrestricted access to the US to plan, support, and conduct future attacks. Thus, AQ is not only recruiting to maintain and expand its global influence to achieve its ideological goals, as discussed in Chapter 2, but is purposefully recruiting people who can avoid counter-terrorism efforts, infiltrate the US, and then prepare for and eventually conduct future attacks.

On several occasions AQ has indicated they want to recruit new members who are not only Arabs, but Muslims of any ethnicity. This statement, when combined with AQ's belief that any of their attacks conducted during this "jihad" are justified based on their extremist interpretations of the Quran, and this presents a very real threat to the US. AQ's extremist interpretation of Islam is used as an effective recruiting tool to attract Muslims, regardless of their nationality or ethnicity. Fortunately, only a small percentage of the Muslim population support this "jihad" or join AQ to carry out acts of violence against anyone they feel are not true believers. Unfortunately, many Muslims who are attracted to AQ's extremist ideology are those who are feel the US's Global War on Terrorism is unfairly targeting Muslim states. Subsequently, these men and women are capable of supporting and carrying out attacks against the US. Therefore, AQ's extremist ideology and recruiting methodologies appeal to people from diverse backgrounds and ethnicities much like Authur Deikmam suggested when he stated, "The motivations of terrorists are diverse, as are their educational and social backgrounds."[51]

This is important for several reasons. First, AQ's extremist ideology and "all source" recruiting methodologies are intended to reach out to any Muslim regardless of their ethnicity to include; men and women of Hispanic, African American, Anglo American, or Asian decent from around the world. The recruitment of these ethnicities, especially those from within the US and EU, exponentially complicates counter-terrorism efforts, and provides AQ with a larger pool of members to organize, train, and recruit. Second, because future recruits may no longer fit current counter-terrorist profiles, they present a greater threat to US National Security, as it will be substantially easier for these AQ members to not only enter the US, but also to blend in with the populous. As J. P. Larsson suggests, "There is no single predictable profile of a potential recruit into terrorist organizations, which has made both law enforcement and research very difficult."[52] Thus, AQ's next generation of potential recruits are being specifically targeted because they can blend in with those they want to attack.

While Larsson's statement is prophetic, there is an even greater threat as AQ appears to be recruiting not only ethnically diverse members but also men and women who have unrestricted access into and within the US. This legitimate access will allow AQ operatives to enter the US and establish themselves as genuine members of American society while covertly establishing and operating AQ cells from within the US. If patient these AQ members will be able to organize, train, recruit, and support AQ operations while simultaneously gaining employment at future target sites.

It is equally important to understand that women are being recruited in order to support and help AQ members blend into mainstream modern US society. Because women are not normally profiled by law enforcement or counter-terrorism agencies it is not difficult to assert that these women, and eventually any grown children from their families, could give AQ even better pre-strike intelligence, detailed planning information, support, and possibly access to targets for future attacks. There have been at least three cases where AQ members and their families have been identified by law enforcement agencies while attempting to blend with the local populist and privately supporting AQ pre-mission activities.[53]

The United Kingdom's recent spat of terrorist attacks is a poignant example of how AQ uses members who can gain access into and within a country, blend with locals, and successfully conduct an attack. Although the UK bombers were of Middle-Eastern decent, because of the diversity of London, they had the ability to blend with local customs, gain extensive knowledge and access to their targets, and then successfully carry out their attacks. More importantly, press reports indicate that the bombers were able to conduct the attacks on their own. If AQ can successfully recruit new members who are ethnically diverse, these new members will be able to blend in with the average American. Similarly, they will have unlimited access into mainstream America. Thus, it is possible that AQ will be able to organize, plan, and execute an attack using similar methodologies to those used in the UK attacks.

Optimally, AQ wants to gain access to high visibility targets whose destruction will produce mass casualties and/or extensive damage to inflict the maximum amount of fear into US citizens. Likely targets include; power production and distribution companies, oil refineries, natural gas and oil distribution companies, chemical production plants, Federal, State, or Local government offices, and any air, rail, or bus transportation facilities. Gaining direct employment with these organizations will give AQ immediate access to the facilities; however, it does not guarantee AQ access to sensitive elements that are critical to the operations of the facilities. If AQ remains patient, and their members can gain the confidence and trust of their supervisors over time, unrestricted access to critical elements of these facilities and companies is a near certainty. AQ does face one major obstacle in gaining employment at these facilities; nearly every employee who works at these organizations must undergo some type of background check.

However, gaining access to these facilities does not mean AQ members have to seek direct employment and risk exposure during background checks. Instead AQ operatives can seek employment with contracted service organizations who have less stringent employment and security requirements, but whose employees have regular access to the same facilities. The inside information gained by either direct hire or contract employees will provide AQ with unprecedented pre-strike intelligence and access to targets when they decide to conduct their attacks. In turn, this access and pre-strike intelligence can optimize the probability of future attacks succeeding while inflicting the maximum amount of damage to critical infrastructure targets.

The bottom line is that AQ recruitment methodologies present a future threat to the US. If AQ can successfully recruit ethnically diverse men and women with legitimate credentials enabling them to enter and remain in the US, it will exponentially increases its chances for conducting successful attacks in the future. Additionally, because future AQ recruits may no longer fit current counter-terrorism profiles, they will present a greater threat, as it will be substantially easier for them to blend in with the populous to conduct pre-strike intelligence, gain access to targets, and carry out attacks. Proof of this threat is apparent in CIA Director Michael Hayden's September 2007 speech when he stated, "We do see them working to train people whom you and I wouldn't raise an eyebrow about if they were getting off the plane with us at Kennedy, people whose identity makes it easier-whose persona makes it easier for them to come into America and to blend into American society."[54]

AU/ACSC/ALLENT/AY08

Chapter 5 – Conclusions and Recommendations

As I have demonstrated, the recruiting methodologies of EITOs are designed to attract new members who can organize, train, support, recruit, and gather funding as well as intelligence, or conduct attacks to help EITOs to achieve their ideological goals. The recruiting efforts of EITOs are conducted 24 hours a day, 365 days of the year, in a variety of physical as well as virtual locations around the world. Based on the case study of the MB and AQ it appears the ideological goals of both organizations are remarkably similar and additional research should indicate other EITOs have similar ideological goals calling for the advancement of Islam and a greater Islamic Nation. Interestingly, EITOs appear to accept anyone, regardless of their ethnicity, as new members to their organizations. EITOs use a combination of active and passive recruiting techniques to replace members who are killed, while simultaneously building the size and capabilities of their organizations to conduct future attacks. Based on these findings and numerous sources, it is likely that AQ is using extremist ideologies to specifically recruit non-traditional Muslims with legitimate access to the US. A plausible scenario detailing how AQ could infiltrate the US and then carry out future attacks was presented earlier in Chapter 4.

Unfortunately, at the unclassified level it appears relatively few studies have been undertaken to fully understand all the different aspects of EITOs recruiting methodologies. While a great deal has been written about terrorism and counter-terrorism topics, recruitment remains a relatively untouched subject. Consequently, almost no formal literature identifies when or why EITOs recruit new members and while some literature does address the other pieces of the analytical puzzle, many conclusions must be inferred from sources which did not intend to address EITOs recruiting methodologies. As such there are several recommended areas for additional research by counter-terrorism analysts using classified and unclassified sources.

Recommendations

First, and foremost, if a detailed examination of the future threat scenario involving AQ has not been accomplished by counter-terrorism analysts it needs to occur as soon as possible. Any findings from that analysis will hopefully help neutralize ongoing AQ efforts to recruit non-traditional Muslims and subsequently infiltrating the US. Additionally, these findings will help develop more accurate terrorist profiles and Indications and Warnings to detect and defeat AQ and other EITO recruiting operations. Second, the full scope of AQ's and other EITO's recruitment methodologies remain undocumented at the unclassified level. If this information is known at the classified level, it needs to be incorporated into the future threat scenario analysis. If this information is not known it needs to be identified as a priority requirement for future analysis using "all-source" intelligence.

Third, a detailed examination and comparison of EITOs ideological goals needs to occur. By understanding what EITOs want to achieve, counter-terrorism efforts can be streamlined to focus on these commonalities. This in turn enables a forth recommendation, which is actually a counter-recruiting strategy. To defeat EITOs, the US must first increase its use of Information Operations (IO) to counter EITO ideologies and recruitment methodologies. This recommendation is meant to persuade national counter-terrorism and political leaders to modify how the US is currently fighting EITOs in the War on Terrorism. IO is a subset of the bigger Information portion of the Diplomatic, Information, Military, and Economic Instruments of Power (IOP) and Information must become the primary IOP used to counter EITO recruiting efforts. The US must develop a better IO campaign to preemptively counter EITOs from using US capitalism, values, and beliefs as recruiting propaganda. This can only be accomplished if the US develops positive IO materials and campaigns for use by legitimate moderate Islamic clerics and leaders to counter EITOs extremist ideologies, especially in prisons, mosques, and universities.

While this paper identifies some the intricacies and dynamics of EITOs recruiting methodologies, using the 6 analytical puzzle pieces, it only scratches the surface of the full scope of EITOs recruiting efforts. Furthermore, attempting to identify what causes men and women to join a terrorist organization is frustrating at best. Authur J. Deikman surmised this dilemma best when he stated, "The motivations of the terrorist are diverse, as are their educational and social backgrounds."[55] However, unless additional detailed and focused analysis is conducted to completely understand EITO recruiting methodologies, and an effort is made to use IO to neutralize them any counter-terrorism efforts aimed at defeating EITOs are destined to fail.

End Notes

[1] United States. Department of State, "Significant Terrorist Incidents 1961-2003: A Brief Chronology," US Government, http://www.state.gov/r/pa/ho/pubs/fs/5902.htm.

[2] United States Deptartment of the Treasury, "Specially Designated Nationals List " US Department of Treasury, http://www.treasury.gov/offices/enforcement/ofac/sdn/sdnlist.txt.

[3] "Profiles of Terrorist Organizations," in *The Making of a Terrorist Recruitment, Training, and Root Causes: Volume One: "Recruitment"*, ed. James J. F. Forest (Westport, CT: Praeger Security International, 2006), 283-342.

[4] Y. H. Aboul-Enein, "Al-Ikhwan Al-Muslimeen: The Muslim Brotherhood," *MILITARY REVIEW* 83 (2003): 92-94.

[5] Ibid.: 27.

[6] Aaron Mannes, "Radical Islam in US Prisons," Profiles in Terror, http://www.profilesinterror.com/updates/2003_12_28_archive.html.

[7] Yonah Alexander, *Middle East Terrorism: Current Threats and Future Prospects* ed. Yonah Alexander, International Library of Terrorism (New York, NY: G.K. Hall, Volume: 5, 1993), 337.

[8] Ziad Munson, "Islamic Mobilization: Social Movement Theory and the Egyptian Muslim Brotherhood," *The Sociological Quarterly* 42, no. 4 (2002): 5.

[9] Abdel Monem Said Aly and Manfred W. Wenner, "Modern Islamic Reform Movements: The Muslim Brotherhood in Contemporary Egypt," *Middle East Journal* 363 (1982): 342.

[10] Munson, "Islamic Mobilization: Social Movement Theory and the Egyptian Muslim Brotherhood," 5.

[11] Aboul-Enein, "Al-Ikhwan Al-Muslimeen: The Muslim Brotherhood," 29.

[12] Guy Arnold, *Revolutionary and Dissident Movements: An International Guide*, 3rd ed. (Harlow: Longman Current Affairs, Distributed exclusively in the USA and Canada by Gale Research Inc., 1991), 72.

[13] John F. Burns, "Remote Yemen May Be Key to Terrorist's Past and Future," http://query.nytimes.com/gst/fullpage.html?res=9B04E7DA1539F936A35752C1A9669C8B63.

[14] Ibid.

[15] Frontline, "A Biography of Osama Bin Laden," PBS, http://www.pbs.org/wgbh/pages/frontline/shows/binladen/who/bio.html.

[16] Michael Scheuer, *Through Our Enemies' Eyes: Osama Bin Laden, Radical Islam, and the Future of America* Revised, 2nd ed. (Washington, D.C.: Potomac Books, Inc., 2006), 93.

[17] Ibid., 92-94.

[18] Ibid., 104-05.

[19] Rohan Gunaratna, "Al Qaeda's Ideology," in *Current Trends in Islamist Ideology. Vol. 1* (Washington, D.C.: Center on Islam, Democracy, and the Future of the Muslim World, Hudson Institute, 2005), 60-61.

[20] Michael Moran, "Bin Laden Comes Home to Roost," MSNBC, http://www.msnbc.msn.com/id/3340101/

[21] Gunaratna, "Al Qaeda's Ideology," 61-62.

[22] David Johnson, "Osama Bin Laden - Wealthy Saudi Exile Is a Terrorist Mastermind," Pearson Education, Inc, http://www.infoplease.com/spot/osamabinladen.html.

[23] Jim Garamone, "Abizaid Details Al Qaeda's Long-Term Goals," American Forces Press Service, http://www.defenselink.mil/news/newsarticle.aspx?id=17178.

[24] Ibid.
[25] Christopher. Henzel, "The Origins of Al Qaeda's Ideology: Implications for US Strategy," *Parameters: Journal of the US Army War College.* 35, no. 1 (2005): 76-77.
[26] Garamone, "Abizaid Details Al Qaeda's Long-Term Goals."
[27] Henzel, "The Origins of Al Qaeda's Ideology: Implications for US Strategy," 76-77.
[28] Christopher M. Blanchard and Service Library of Congress. Congressional Research, "Al Qaeda Statements and Evolving Ideology," Congressional Research Service, http://www.fas.org/sgp/crs/terror/RL32759.pdf
[29] Garamone, "Abizaid Details Al Qaeda's Long-Term Goals."
[30] "Muslim Brotherhood Movement Homepage," http://www.ummah.net/ikhwan/.
[31] Ibid.
[32] Blanchard and Library of Congress. Congressional Research, "Al Qaeda Statements and Evolving Ideology."
[33] Cindy C. Combs, "The Media as a Showcase for Terrorism," in *Teaching Terror: Strategic and Tactical Learning in the Terrorist World* ed. James J. F. Forest (Lanham, MD: Rowman & Littlefield, 2006), 142.
[34] Lubomir Bistrekov, "Islamist Recruitment Mechanisms in Europe: Understanding and Countering a Growing Threat," in *A Report on Counter Terrorism Working Group Report Zurich September 2005* (Zurich, Switzerland: Partnership for Peace Consortium of Defense Academics and Security Studies Institutes, 2005).
[35] Justice United States. Dept. of, "The Al Qaeda Training Manual," in *Military Studies in the Jihad Against the Tyrants:*, ed. Jerrold M. Post (Maxwell Air Force Base, AL: USAF Counterproliferation Center), 1-175.
[36] Marc Sageman, *Understanding Terror Networks* (Philadelphia, PA: University of Pennsylvania Press, 2004), 123.
[37] Combs, "The Media as a Showcase for Terrorism," 141-47.
[38] Souad Mekhennet and Michael Moss, "Europeans Get Terror Training Inside Pakistan," *New York Times*, 10 September 2007.
[39] Sageman, *Understanding Terror Networks* 161.
[40] Jessica Stern, *Terror in the Name of God Why Religious Militants Kill* (New York, NY: Ecco, 2003), 258-59.
[41] Senate Judiciary Committee, Subcommitte on Terrorism, Technology, and Homeland Security, *Terrorist Recruitment in Prisons and the Recent Arrests Related to Guantanamo Bay Detainees* 14 October 2003.
[42] United States Senate Judiciary Committee on the Judiciary: Subcommittee on Terrorism, Technology, and Homeland Security, *Terrorist Recruitment and Infiltration in the United States: Prisons and Military as an Operational Base* 14 October 2003.
[43] Ibid.
[44] Michael J. Waller, "Prisons as Terrorist Breeding Grounds," in *The Making of a Terrorist Recruitment, Training, and Root Causes: Volume One: "Recruitment"*, ed. James J. F. Forest (Westport, CT: Praeger Security International, 2006), 34.
[45] Quintan Wiktorowicz, *The Management of Islamic Activism: Salafis, the Muslim Brotherhood, and State Power in Jordan* Suny Series in Middle East Studies (Albany, NY: State University of New York Press, 2001), 52.
[46] Stern, *Terror in the Name of God Why Religious Militants Kill*, 259.

[47] Robert Winnett and David Leppard, "Leaked No 10 Dossier Reveals Al-Qaeda's British Recruits," *The Times Online*, 10 July 2005.

[48] United States. Dept. of, "The Al Qaeda Training Manual," 25.

[49] Sageman, *Understanding Terror Networks* 122.

[50] Arthur J. Deikman, "The Psychological Power of Charismatic Leaders in Cults and Terrorist Organizations," in *The Making of a Terrorist Recruitment, Training, and Root Causes: Volume Two: "Training"*, ed. James J. F. Forest (Westport, CT: Praeger Security International, 2006), 82.

[51] Ibid.

[52] J. P. Larsson, "The Role of Religious Ideology in Modern Terrorist Recruitment," in *The Making of a Terrorist Recruitment, Training, and Root Causes: Volume One: "Recruitment"*, ed. James J. F. Forest (Westport, CT: Praeger Security International, 2006), 199.

[53] Daniel Klaidman et al., "Al Qaeda in America: The Enemy Within," *Newsweek*, 23 June 2003.

[54] Mekhennet and Moss, "Europeans Get Terror Training Inside Pakistan," 2.

[55] Deikman, "The Psychological Power of Charismatic Leaders in Cults and Terrorist Organizations," 82.

Bibliography

Abb, Madelfia A., and Cindy R. Jebb. "Human Security and Good Governance: A Living Systems Approach to Understanding and Combating Terrorism." In *The Making of a Terrorist Recruitment, Training, and Root Causes: Volume Three: "Root Causes"*, edited by James J. F. Forest, 220-37. Westport, CT: Praeger Security International, 2006.

Abbas, Hassan. "A Failure to Communicate: American Public Diplomacy in the Islamic World." In *The Making of a Terrorist Recruitment, Training, and Root Causes: Volume Three: "Root Causes"*, edited by James J. F. Forest, 45-61. Westport, CT: Praeger Security International, 2006.

Aboul-Enein, Y. H. "Al-Ikhwan Al-Muslimeen: The Muslim Brotherhood." *MILITARY REVIEW* 83 (2003): 26-31.

Abuza, Zachary. "Education and Radicalization: Jemaah Isamiyah Recruitment in Southeast Asia." In *The Making of a Terrorist Recruitment, Training, and Root Causes: Volume One: "Recruitment"*, edited by James J. F. Forest, 66-83. Westport, CT: Praeger Security International, 2006.

Ahmad, Eqbal. "Terrorism: Theirs & Ours." In *Terrorism and Counterterrorism Understanding the New Security Environment: Readings & Interpretations*, edited by Russell D. Howard and Reid L. Sawyer, 46-52. Guilford, CT: McGraw-Hill Companies, 2002.

Ahmed-Ullah, Noreen S., Sam Roe, and Laurie Cohen. "A Rare Look at Secretive Brotherhood in America." *Chicago Tribune*, 19 September 2004

"Al Qaeda Declaration of War." In *The Making of a Terrorist Recruitment, Training, and Root Causes: Volume One: "Recruitment"*, edited by James J. F. Forest, 343-68. Westport, CT: Praeger Security International, 2006.

Alexander, Yonah. *Middle East Terrorism: Current Threats and Future Prospects* Edited by Yonah Alexander, International Library of Terrorism. New York, NY: G.K. Hall, Volume: 5, 1993.

Ami, Pedahzu, and Arie Perliger. "The Making of Suicide Bombers: A Comparative Perspective." In *The Making of a Terrorist Recruitment, Training, and Root Causes: Volume One: "Recruitment"*, edited by James J. F. Forest, 151-64. Westport, CT: Praeger Security International, 2006.

Arnold, Guy. *Revolutionary and Dissident Movements: An International Guide*. 3rd ed. Harlow: Longman Current Affairs, Distributed exclusively in the USA and Canada by Gale Research Inc., 1991.

Arquilla, John, David Ronfeldt, and Michele Zanini. "Networks, Netwar, and Information-Age Terrorism." In *Terrorism and Counterterrorism Understanding the New Security Environment: Readings & Interpretations*, edited by Russell D. Howard and Reid L. Sawyer, 86-108. Guilford, CT: McGraw-Hill Companies, 2002.

Azzam, Maha. "Political Islam: Violence and the Wahhabi Connection." In *The Making of a Terrorist Recruitment, Training, and Root Causes: Volume One: "Recruitment"*, edited by James J. F. Forest, 232-45. Westport, CT: Praeger Security International, 2006.

Bandura, Albert. "Training for Terrorism Throught Selective Moral Disengagement." In *The Making of a Terrorist Recruitment, Training, and Root Causes: Volume Two: "Training"*, edited by James J. F. Forest, 34-50. Westport, CT: Praeger Security International, 2006.

Barkun, Michael. "Terrorism and Doomsday." In *The Making of a Terrorist Recruitment, Training, and Root Causes: Volume Three: "Root Causes"*, edited by James J. F. Forest, 126-39. Westport, CT: Praeger Security International, 2006.

Barsky, Yehudit, Alan M. Schwartz, and League B'Nai B'rith. Anti-Defamation. *Hamas, Islamic Jihad and the Muslim Brotherhood Islamic Extremists and the Terrorist Threat to America*. New York, NY: Anti-Defamation League, 1993.

Beitler, Ruth Margolies. "The Complex Relationship between Global Terrorism and US Support for Israel." In *The Making of a Terrorist Recruitment, Training, and Root Causes: Volume Three: "Root Causes"*, edited by James J. F. Forest, 62-73. Westport, CT: Praeger Security International, 2006.

Betts, Richard K. "Fixing Intelligence." In *Terrorism and Counterterrorism Understanding the New Security Environment: Readings & Interpretations*, edited by Russell D. Howard and Reid L. Sawyer, 459-69. Guilford, CT: McGraw-Hill Companies, 2002.

———. "Soft Underbelly of American Primacy: Tactical Advantages of Terror." In *Terrorism and Counterterrorism Understanding the New Security Environment: Readings & Interpretations*, edited by Russell D. Howard and Reid L. Sawyer, 376-91. Guilford, CT: McGraw-Hill Companies, 2002.

Binyon, Michael "Why Medical Schools Provide Islamic Extremists with Fertile Recruiting Grounds." *The Times Online*, 4 July 2007.

Bistrekov, Lubomir. "Islamist Recruitment Mechanisms in Europe: Understanding and Countering a Growing Threat." In *A Report on Counter Terrorism Working Group Report Zurich September 2005*. Zurich, Switzerland: Partnership for Peace Consortium of Defense Academics and Security Studies Institutes, 2005.

Blanchard, Christopher M., and Service Library of Congress. Congressional Research. "Al Qaeda Statements and Evolving Ideology." Congressional Research Service, http://www.fas.org/sgp/crs/terror/RL32759.pdf

Brachman, Jarret. "Jihad Doctrine and Radical Islam." In *The Making of a Terrorist Recruitment, Training, and Root Causes: Volume One: "Recruitment"*, edited by James J. F. Forest, 246-59. Westport, CT: Praeger Security International, 2006.

Burke, Jason. *Al-Qaeda : The True Story of Radical Islam*. New York, NY: I.B. Tauris & Co Ltd, 2004.

———. *Al-Qaeda: Casting a Shadow of Terror*. New York, NY: I. B. Tauris & Co Ltd, 2003.

Burns, John F. "Remote Yemen May Be Key to Terrorist's Past and Future." http://query.nytimes.com/gst/fullpage.html?res=9B04E7DA1539F936A35752C1A9669C8B63.

Byman, Daniel. *Trends in Outside Support for Insurgent Movements* Santa Monica, CA: Rand, 2001.

Chenoweth, Erica. "Instability and Opportunity: The Origins of Terrorism in Weak and Failing States." In *The Making of a Terrorist Recruitment, Training, and Root Causes: Volume Three: "Root Causes"*, edited by James J. F. Forest, 17-30. Westport, CT: Praeger Security International, 2006.

Cilluffo, Frank J. "Out of the Shadows Getting Ahead of Prisoner Radicalization: A Special Report." George Washington University Homeland Security Policy Institute, University of Virginia. Critical Incident Analysis, Group, http://homelandsecurity.gwu.edu/reports/rad/Out%20of%20the%20shadows.pdf

Coffin, McKinley D. "Prison Radicalization the New Extremist Training Grounds?" Naval Postgraduate School, 2007.

Combs, Cindy C. "The Media as a Showcase for Terrorism." In *Teaching Terror: Strategic and Tactical Learning in the Terrorist World* edited by James J. F. Forest, 133-54. Lanham, MD: Rowman & Littlefield, 2006.

Conway, Maura. "Terrorism and It: Cyberterrorism and Terrorist Organisations Online." In *Terrorism and Counterterrorism Understanding the New Security Environment: Readings & Interpretations*, edited by Russell D. Howard and Reid L. Sawyer, 271-88. Guilford, CT: McGraw-Hill Companies, 2002.

Coolsaet, Rik. *Between Al-Andalus and a Failing Integration: Europe's Pursuit of a Long-Term Counterterrorism Strategy in the Post-Al-Qaeda Era*. Gent: Acad. Press, 2005.

Corson, Adrienne M., and Studies Missouri State University. Dept. of Defense and Strategic. "Hizb Ut-Tahrir Preemptively Eradicating the Recruitment Pool for Radical Islamic Terrorist Organizations." 2006.

Cozzens, Jeffrey. "Terrorism and Insurgency - Islamic Groups Develop New Recruiting Strategies." *Jane's Intelligence Review* 17, no. 2 (2005): 22.

Cragin, Kim, Intelligence United States. Congress. Senate. Select Committee on, and Corporation Rand. "Understanding Terrorist Ideology." RAND, http://www.rand.org/pubs/testimonies/2007/RAND_CT283.pdf

Cragin, Kim R. "Learning to Survive: The Case of the Islamic Resistance." In *Teaching Terror: Strategic and Tactical Learning in the Terrorist World* edited by James J. F. Forest, 189-204. Lanham, MD: Rowman & Littlefield, 2006.

Crenshaw, Martha. "Counterterrorism Policy and the Political Process." In *Terrorism and Counterterrorism Understanding the New Security Environment: Readings & Interpretations*, edited by Russell D. Howard and Reid L. Sawyer, 450-58. Guilford, CT: McGraw-Hill Companies, 2002.

———. "The Logic of Terrorism: Terrorist Behavior as a Product of Strategic Choice." In *Terrorism and Counterterrorism Understanding the New Security Environment: Readings & Interpretations*, edited by Russell D. Howard and Reid L. Sawyer, 54-66. Guilford, CT: McGraw-Hill Companies, 2002.

Deikman, Arthur J. "The Psychological Power of Charismatic Leaders in Cults and Terrorist Organizations." In *The Making of a Terrorist Recruitment, Training, and Root Causes: Volume Two: "Training"*, edited by James J. F. Forest, 71-83. Westport, CT: Praeger Security International, 2006.

Department of State, United States. "Significant Terrorist Incidents 1961-2003: A Brief Chronology." US Government, http://www.state.gov/r/pa/ho/pubs/fs/5902.htm.

Dolnik, Adam. "Learning to Die: Suicide Terrorism in the Twenty-First Century." In *The Making of a Terrorist Recruitment, Training, and Root Causes: Volume Two: "Training"*, edited by James J. F. Forest, 152-71. Westport, CT: Praeger Security International, 2006.

Donahue, Laura K. "Fear Itself: Counterterrorism, Individual Rights, and U.S. Foreign Relations Post 9-11." In *Terrorism and Counterterrorism Understanding the New Security Environment: Readings & Interpretations*, edited by Russell D. Howard and Reid L. Sawyer, 313-38. Guilford, CT: McGraw-Hill Companies, 2002.

Ehrlich, Paul R., and Jiangui Liu. "Socioeconomic and Demographic Roots of Terrorism." In *The Making of a Terrorist Recruitment, Training, and Root Causes: Volume Three: "Root*

Causes", edited by James J. F. Forest, 160-71. Westport, CT: Praeger Security International, 2006.

Ellis, Brent. "Countering Complexity: An Analytical Framework to Guide Counter-Terrorism Policy Making." In *Terrorism and Counterterrorism Understanding the New Security Environment: Readings & Interpretations*, edited by Russell D. Howard and Reid L. Sawyer, 109-22. Guilford, CT: McGraw-Hill Companies, 2002.

Ellis, John. "Terrorism in the Genomic Age." In *Terrorism and Counterterrorism Understanding the New Security Environment: Readings & Interpretations*, edited by Russell D. Howard and Reid L. Sawyer, 303-09. Guilford, CT: McGraw-Hill Companies, 2002.

Emerson, Steven. *American Jihad: Terrorists Living Among Us*. New York, NY: Free Press, 2002.

Europol. "Eu Terrorism Situation and Trend Report 2007." In *TE-SAT 2007*. Hague, Netherlands: Europol, 2007.

Farah, Douglas, Ron Sandee, and Josh Lefkowitz. "The Muslim Brotherhood in the United States: A Brief History." The Nine/Eleven Finding Answers Foundation, http://www.nefafoundation.org/miscellaneous/nefaikhwan1007.pdf.

Felbab-Brown, Vanda. "The Intersection of Terrorism and the Drug Trade." In *The Making of a Terrorist Recruitment, Training, and Root Causes: Volume Three: "Root Causes"*, edited by James J. F. Forest, 172-88. Westport, CT: Praeger Security International, 2006.

Felter, Joseph. "Recruitment for Rebellion and Terrorism in the Philippines." In *The Making of a Terrorist Recruitment, Training, and Root Causes: Volume One: "Recruitment"*, edited by James J. F. Forest, 84-104. Westport, CT: Praeger Security International, 2006.

Forest, James J. F. "Conclusion." In *Teaching Terror: Strategic and Tactical Learning in the Terrorist World* edited by James J. F. Forest, 261-72. Lanham, MD: Rowman & Littlefield, 2006.

———. "Exploring Root Causes of Terrorism: An Introduction." In *The Making of a Terrorist Recruitment, Training, and Root Causes: Volume Three: "Root Causes"*, edited by James J. F. Forest, 1-16. Westport, CT: Praeger Security International, 2006.

———. "Exploring the Recruitment of Terrorists: An Introduction." In *The Making of a Terrorist Recruitment, Training, and Root Causes: Volume One: "Recruitment"*, edited by James J. F. Forest, 1-9. Westport, CT: Praeger Security International, 2006.

———. "Exploring the Training of Terrorists: An Introduction." In *The Making of a Terrorist Recruitment, Training, and Root Causes: Volume Two: "Training"*, edited by James J. F. Forest, 1-12. Westport, CT: Praeger Security International, 2006.

———. "Introduction." In *Teaching Terror: Strategic and Tactical Learning in the Terrorist World* edited by James J. F. Forest, 1-32. Lanham, MD: Rowman & Littlefield, 2006.

———. *The Making of a Terrorist Recruitment, Training, and Root Causes: Volume One: "Recruitment"*. Edited by James J. F. Forest. Westport, CT: Praeger Security International, 2006.

———. *The Making of a Terrorist Recruitment, Training, and Root Causes: Volume Three: "Root Causes"*. Edited by James J. F. Forest. Westport, CT: Praeger Security International, 2006.

———. *The Making of a Terrorist Recruitment, Training, and Root Causes: Volume Two: "Training"*. Edited by James J. F. Forest. Westport, CT: Praeger Security International, 2006.

———. *Teaching Terror: Strategic and Tactical Learning in the Terrorist World* Edited by James J. F. Forest. Lanham, MD: Rowman & Littlefield, 2006.

———. "Teaching Terrorism: Dimensions of Information and Technology." In *The Making of a Terrorist Recruitment, Training, and Root Causes: Volume Two: "Training"*, edited by James J. F. Forest, 84-97. Westport, CT: Praeger Security International, 2006.

———. "Terrorist Training Centers around the World: A Brief Review." In *The Making of a Terrorist Recruitment, Training, and Root Causes: Volume Two: "Training"*, edited by James J. F. Forest, 296-310. Westport, CT: Praeger Security International, 2006.

———. "Training Camps and Other Centers of Learning:." In *Teaching Terror: Strategic and Tactical Learning in the Terrorist World* edited by James J. F. Forest, 69-109. Lanham, MD: Rowman & Littlefield, 2006.

Frontline. "A Biography of Osama Bin Laden." PBS, http://www.pbs.org/wgbh/pages/frontline/shows/binladen/who/bio.html.

Galanter, Marc, and James J. F. Forest. "Cults, Charismatic Groups, and Social Systems: Understanding the Transformation of Terrorist Recruits." In *The Making of a Terrorist Recruitment, Training, and Root Causes: Volume Two: "Training"*, edited by James J. F. Forest, 51-70. Westport, CT: Praeger Security International, 2006.

Ganor, Boaz, Katharina Von Knop, and Carlos Duarte. *Hypermedia Seduction for Terrorist Recruiting*. Edited by Boaz Ganor, Katharina Von Knop and Carlos. Duarte, NATO Advanced Research Workshop on Hypermedia Seduction for Terrorist Recruiting. Amsterdam, Netherlands; Washington, DC: IOS Press in cooperation with NATO Public Diplomacy Division, 2007.

Garamone, Jim. "Abizaid Details Al Qaeda's Long-Term Goals." American Forces Press Service, http://www.defenselink.mil/news/newsarticle.aspx?id=17178.

Gruen, Madeline. "Innovative Recruitment and Indoctrination Tactics by Extremists: Video Games, Hip-Hop, and the World Wide Web." In *The Making of a Terrorist Recruitment, Training, and Root Causes: Volume One: "Recruitment"*, edited by James J. F. Forest, 11-22. Westport, CT: Praeger Security International, 2006.

———. "White Ethnonationalist and Political Islamist Methods of Fundraising and Propaganda on the Internet." In *Terrorism and Counterterrorism Understanding the New Security Environment: Readings & Interpretations*, edited by Russell D. Howard and Reid L. Sawyer, 289-302. Guilford, CT: McGraw-Hill Companies, 2002.

Gunaratna, Rohan. "Al Qaeda's Ideology." In *Current Trends in Islamist Ideology. Vol. 1* 59-67. Washington, D.C.: Center on Islam, Democracy, and the Future of the Muslim World, Hudson Institute, 2005.

———. "Al Qaeda's Lose and Learn Doctrine: The Trajectory from Oplan Bojinka to 9/11." In *Teaching Terror: Strategic and Tactical Learning in the Terrorist World* edited by James J. F. Forest, 171-88. Lanham, MD: Rowman & Littlefield, 2006.

Gunaratna, Rohan, and Arabinda Acharya. "The Terrorist Training Camps of Al Qaeda." In *The Making of a Terrorist Recruitment, Training, and Root Causes: Volume Two: "Training"*, edited by James J. F. Forest, 172-93. Westport, CT: Praeger Security International, 2006.

Hafez, Mohammed M. "Political Repression and Violent Rebellion in the Muslim World." In *The Making of a Terrorist Recruitment, Training, and Root Causes: Volume Three: "Root Causes"*, edited by James J. F. Forest, 74-91. Westport, CT: Praeger Security International, 2006.

Halaburda, Pablo. "Terrorism Base Potential in the Tri-Border Area of Latin America." Naval Postgraduate School, 2006.

Hamden, Raymond H. "Unresolved Trauma and the Thirst for Revenge: The Retributional Terrorist." In *The Making of a Terrorist Recruitment, Training, and Root Causes: Volume One: "Recruitment"*, edited by James J. F. Forest, 165-80. Westport, CT: Praeger Security International, 2006.

Henzel, Christopher. "The Origins of Al Qaeda's Ideology: Implications for US Strategy." *Parameters: Journal of the US Army War College*. 35, no. 1 (2005): 69-80.

Hippel, Karin von. "Dealing with the Roots of Terror." In *The Making of a Terrorist Recruitment, Training, and Root Causes: Volume Three: "Root Causes"*, edited by James J. F. Forest, 266-76. Westport, CT: Praeger Security International, 2006.

Hoffmann, Bruce. "Defining Terrorism." In *Terrorism and Counterterrorism Understanding the New Security Environment: Readings & Interpretations*, edited by Russell D. Howard and Reid L. Sawyer, 3-23. Guilford, CT: McGraw-Hill Companies, 2002.

———. "A Nasty Business." In *Terrorism and Counterterrorism Understanding the New Security Environment: Readings & Interpretations*, edited by Russell D. Howard and Reid L. Sawyer, 339-44. Guilford, CT: McGraw-Hill Companies, 2002.

Horne, Alistair. "Roots of Terror - the New Jihad Can Be Traced Back to Algeria 50 Years Ago." *The Spectator* (2004): 28.

Howard, Russell D. "Understanding Al Qaeda's Application of the New Terrorism-the Key to Victory in the Current Campaign." In *Terrorism and Counterterrorism Understanding the New Security Environment: Readings & Interpretations*, edited by Russell D. Howard and Reid L. Sawyer, 75-85. Guilford, CT: McGraw-Hill Companies, 2002.

Howard, Russell D., and Reid L. Sawyer. "Background Information on Designated Foreign Terrorist Organizations." In *Terrorism and Counterterrorism Understanding the New Security Environment: Readings & Interpretations*, edited by Russell D. Howard and Reid L. Sawyer, 503-27. Guilford, CT: McGraw-Hill Companies, 2002.

———. "Significant Terrorism Incidents, 1961-2001." In *Terrorism and Counterterrorism Understanding the New Security Environment: Readings & Interpretations*, edited by Russell D. Howard and Reid L. Sawyer, 528-83. Guilford, CT: McGraw-Hill Companies, 2002.

———. *Terrorism and Counterterrorism Understanding the New Security Environment: Readings & Interpretations*. Guilford, CT: McGraw-Hill Companies, 2002.

Hudson, Rex A. "The Sociology and Psychology of Terrorism: Who Becomes a Terrorist and Why?" Defense Technical Information Center, Library Of Congress Washington DC Federal Research, D. I. V., http://handle.dtic.mil/100.2/ADA442836

Ibrahim, Raymond, Ayman Zawahiri, and Osama Bin Laden. *The Al Qaeda Reader*. Translated by Raymond Ibrahim. Edited by Raymond Ibrahim. New York, NY: Doubleday, 2007.

Imm, Jeffery. "Al Qaeda Seeks Ties to Dc Gangs." *Washington Times*, 1 October 2004 2004.

Jackson, Michael J., and Wayne R. Lacey. "Homegrown Terror the United Kingdom as a Case Study." Naval Postgraduate School, 2007.

Johnson, David. "Osama Bin Laden - Wealthy Saudi Exile Is a Terrorist Mastermind." Pearson Education, Inc, http://www.infoplease.com/spot/osamabinladen.html.

Juergensmeyer, Mark. "The Logic of Religious Violence." In *Terrorism and Counterterrorism Understanding the New Security Environment: Readings & Interpretations*, edited by

Russell D. Howard and Reid L. Sawyer, 140-58. Guilford, CT: McGraw-Hill Companies, 2002.

Justice, United States Deptartment of. "The Al Qaeda Training Manual." In *Military Studies in the Jihad Against the Tyrants: The Al Qaeda Training Manual*, edited by Jerrold M. Post, 175. Maxwell Air Force Base, AL: USAF Counterproliferation Center.

Kamien, David G. *The Mcgraw-Hill Homeland Security Handbook*. New York, NY: McGraw-Hill, 2006.

Kenney, Michael. "How Terrorists Learn." In *Teaching Terror: Strategic and Tactical Learning in the Terrorist World* edited by James J. F. Forest, 33-51. Lanham, MD: Rowman & Littlefield, 2006.

Klaidman, Daniel, Mark Hosenball, Michael Isikoff, and Evan Thomas. "Al Qaeda in America: The Enemy Within." *Newsweek*, 23 June 2003.

Klare, Michael T. "Fueling the Fires: The Oil Factor in Middle Eastern Terrorism." In *The Making of a Terrorist Recruitment, Training, and Root Causes: Volume Three: "Root Causes"*, edited by James J. F. Forest, 140-59. Westport, CT: Praeger Security International, 2006.

Kohlmann, Evan. "The Mujahideen of Bosnia: Origins, Training and Implications." In *The Making of a Terrorist Recruitment, Training, and Root Causes: Volume Two: "Training"*, edited by James J. F. Forest, 194-210. Westport, CT: Praeger Security International, 2006.

Larsson, J. P. "The Role of Religious Ideology in Modern Terrorist Recruitment." In *The Making of a Terrorist Recruitment, Training, and Root Causes: Volume One: "Recruitment"*, edited by James J. F. Forest, 197-215. Westport, CT: Praeger Security International, 2006.

Lefkowitz, Josh. "The 1993 Philadelphia Meeting: A Roadmap for Furture Mulim Brotherhood Actions in the U.S." The Nine/Eleven Finding Answers Foundation, http://www.nefafoundation.org/miscellaneous/93Phillyfinal.pdf.

Levitt, Matthew A. "Hamas Social Welfare: In the Service of Terror." In *The Making of a Terrorist Recruitment, Training, and Root Causes: Volume One: "Recruitment"*, edited by James J. F. Forest, 120-35. Westport, CT: Praeger Security International, 2006.

Liotta, P. H., and James F. Miskel. "Digging Deep: Environment and Geography as Root Influences for Terrorism." In *The Making of a Terrorist Recruitment, Training, and Root Causes: Volume Three: "Root Causes"*, edited by James J. F. Forest, 254-65. Westport, CT: Praeger Security International, 2006.

Mannes, Aaron. "Radical Islam in US Prisons." Profiles in Terror, http://www.profilesinterror.com/updates/2003_12_28_archive.html.

Marks, Alexandra. "Arrests of a Maryland Paramedic and a Possible Terror-Camp Organizer Raise New Security Concerns." *The Christian Science Monitor* (2005).

McCaffrey, Barry R., and John A. Basso. "Narcotics, Terrorisms, and International Crime: The Convergence Phenomenon." In *Terrorism and Counterterrorism Understanding the New Security Environment: Readings & Interpretations*, edited by Russell D. Howard and Reid L. Sawyer, 245-59. Guilford, CT: McGraw-Hill Companies, 2002.

McCauley, Clark R. "Terrorism and the State: The Logic of Killing Civilians." In *The Making of a Terrorist Recruitment, Training, and Root Causes: Volume Three: "Root Causes"*, edited by James J. F. Forest, 238-53. Westport, CT: Praeger Security International, 2006.

Mekhennet, Souad, and Michael Moss. "Europeans Get Terror Training Inside Pakistan." *New York Times*, 10 September 2007.

Mitchell, Richard P. *The Society of the Muslim Brothers*. Vol. 9, Middle Eastern Monographs. London, England: Oxford University Press, 1969.

Moran, Michael. "Bin Laden Comes Home to Roost." MSNBC, http://www.msnbc.msn.com/id/3340101/

Munson, Ziad. "Islamic Mobilization: Social Movement Theory and the Egyptian Muslim Brotherhood." *The Sociological Quarterly* 42, no. 4 (2002): 40.

Murphy, Dan. "Southeast Asia Easy Source of Al Qaeda Recruits." *The Christian Science Monitor* 94, no. 222 (2002): 7.

Musallam, Adnan. *From Secularism to Jihad : Sayyid Qutb and the Foundations of Radical Islamism*. Westport, CT: Praeger, 2005.

"Muslim Brotherhood Movement Homepage." http://www.ummah.net/ikhwan/.

Myers, Richard B. *National Military Strategic Plan for the War on Terrorism*. Washington, D.C.: Chairman of the Joint Chiefs of Staff, 2006.

Nacos, Brigitte L. "Communication and Recruitment of Terrorists." In *The Making of a Terrorist Recruitment, Training, and Root Causes: Volume One: "Recruitment"*, edited by James J. F. Forest, 41-52. Westport, CT: Praeger Security International, 2006.

———. "Meditated Terror: Teaching Terrorism Trhought Propaganda." In *The Making of a Terrorist Recruitment, Training, and Root Causes: Volume Two: "Training"*, edited by James J. F. Forest, 98-117. Westport, CT: Praeger Security International, 2006.

National Security, Council. "9/11 Five Years Later Successes and Challenges." National Security Council, http://purl.access.gpo.gov/GPO/LPS74418

———. "National Strategy for Combating Terrorism." National Security Council, http://purl.access.gpo.gov/GPO/LPS74421

Olcott, Martha Brill, and Bakhtiyar Babajanov. "Teaching New Terrorist Recruits: A Review of Training Manuals Fromthe Uzbekistan Mujahideen." In *The Making of a Terrorist Recruitment, Training, and Root Causes: Volume Two: "Training"*, edited by James J. F. Forest, 136-51. Westport, CT: Praeger Security International, 2006.

Ortiz, Roman D. "The Human Factor in Insurgency: Recruitment and Training in the Revolutionary Armed Forces of Columbia (Farc)." In *The Making of a Terrorist Recruitment, Training, and Root Causes: Volume Two: "Training"*, edited by James J. F. Forest, 263-76. Westport, CT: Praeger Security International, 2006.

———. "Renew to Last: Innovation and Strategy of the Revolutionary Armed Forces of Columbia." In *Teaching Terror: Strategic and Tactical Learning in the Terrorist World* edited by James J. Forest, 205-23. Lanham, MD: Rowman & Littlefield, 2006.

Pearce, Susanna. "Religious Sources of Violence." In *The Making of a Terrorist Recruitment, Training, and Root Causes: Volume Three: "Root Causes"*, edited by James J. F. Forest, 109-25. Westport, CT: Praeger Security International, 2006.

Phares, Walid. *Future Jihad Terrorist Strategies Against America*. New York, NY: Palgrave Macmillan, 2005.

———. *The War of Ideas: Jihad Against Democracy*. 1st ed. ed. New York, NY: Palgrave Macmillan, 2007.

Pillar, Paul R. "The Dimensions of Terrorism and Counterterrorism." In *Terrorism and Counterterrorism Understanding the New Security Environment: Readings &*

Interpretations, edited by Russell D. Howard and Reid L. Sawyer, 24-45. Guilford, CT: McGraw-Hill Companies, 2002.

———. "Superpower Foreign Policies: A Source for Global Resentment." In *The Making of a Terrorist Recruitment, Training, and Root Causes: Volume Three: "Root Causes"*, edited by James J. F. Forest, 31-44. Westport, CT: Praeger Security International, 2006.

Posen, Barry R. "The Struggle Against Terrorism: Grand Strategy, Strategy, and Tactics." In *Terrorism and Counterterrorism Understanding the New Security Environment: Readings & Interpretations*, edited by Russell D. Howard and Reid L. Sawyer, 429-41. Guilford, CT: McGraw-Hill Companies, 2002.

Post, Jerrold M. ""When Hatred Is Bred in the Bone": The Sociocultural Underpinnings of Terrorist Psychology." In *The Making of a Terrorist Recruitment, Training, and Root Causes: Volume Two: "Training"*, edited by James J. F. Forest, 13-33. Westport, CT: Praeger Security International, 2006.

"Profiles of Terrorist Organizations." In *The Making of a Terrorist Recruitment, Training, and Root Causes: Volume One: "Recruitment"*, edited by James J. F. Forest, 283-342. Westport, CT: Praeger Security International, 2006.

Rabasa, Angel, and C. A. Rand Corp Santa Monica. "Moderate and Radical Islam." Defense Technical Information Center, http://handle.dtic.mil/100.2/ADA440170

Ramakrishna, Kumar. "Indoctrination Processes within Jemaah Islamiyah." In *The Making of a Terrorist Recruitment, Training, and Root Causes: Volume Two: "Training"*, edited by James J. F. Forest, 211-25. Westport, CT: Praeger Security International, 2006.

———. "The Making of the Jemaah Islamiyah Terrorist." In *Teaching Terror: Strategic and Tactical Learning in the Terrorist World* edited by James J. F. Forest, 223-60. Lanham, MD: Rowman & Littlefield, 2006.

Ranstorp, Magnus. "The Hizballah Training Camps of Lebanon." In *The Making of a Terrorist Recruitment, Training, and Root Causes: Volume Two: "Training"*, edited by James J. F. Forest, 243-63. Westport, CT: Praeger Security International, 2006.

———. "Terrorism in the Name of Religion." In *Terrorism and Counterterrorism Understanding the New Security Environment: Readings & Interpretations*, edited by Russell D. Howard and Reid L. Sawyer, 125-39. Guilford, CT: McGraw-Hill Companies, 2002.

Rice-Oxley, Mark. "Home-Grown Terrorist Recruitment Rising, Says British Spy Chiefs." *The Christian Science Monitor* (2007).

Richardson, Louise E. "Global Rebels: Terrorist Organizations as Trans-National Actors." In *Terrorism and Counterterrorism Understanding the New Security Environment: Readings & Interpretations*, edited by Russell D. Howard and Reid L. Sawyer, 67-73. Guilford, CT: McGraw-Hill Companies, 2002.

Robbins, James S. "Bin Laden's War." In *Terrorism and Counterterrorism Understanding the New Security Environment: Readings & Interpretations*, edited by Russell D. Howard and Reid L. Sawyer, 392-404. Guilford, CT: McGraw-Hill Companies, 2002.

Rosenau, W. "Al Qaida Recruitment Trends in Kenya and Tanzania." *Violence & Abuse Abstracts* 11, no. 3 (2005).

Sageman, Marc. *Understanding Terror Networks* Philadelphia, PA: University of Pennsylvania Press, 2004.

Said Aly, Abdel Monem, and Manfred W. Wenner. "Modern Islamic Reform Movements: The Muslim Brotherhood in Contemporary Egypt." *Middle East Journal* 363 (1982): 336-61.

Saudi Arabia's Al-Turki Says Terrorists Recruit Youth for Technological Skills. World News Connection.

Scheuer, Michael. *Through Our Enemies' Eyes: Osama Bin Laden, Radical Islam, and the Future of America* Revised, 2nd ed. Washington, D.C.: Potomac Books, Inc., 2006.

Schneider, Barry R., Jerrold M. Post, and USAF Counterproliferation Center. *Know Thy Enemy: Profiles of Adversary Leaders and Their Strategic Cultures*. Maxwell Air Force Base, AL Wash. D.C.: USAF Counterproliferation Center ; For sale by the Supt. of Docs., G.P.O., 2003.

Schultz, Richard H., and Andreas Vogt. "The Real Intelligence Failure on 9/11 and the Case for a Doctrine of Striking First." In *Terrorism and Counterterrorism Understanding the New Security Environment: Readings & Interpretations*, edited by Russell D. Howard and Reid L. Sawyer, 405-28. Guilford, CT: McGraw-Hill Companies, 2002.

Senate Judiciary Committee, Subcommitte on Terrorism, Technology, and Homeland Security. *Terrorist Recruitment in Prisons and the Recent Arrests Related to Guantanamo Bay Detainees* 14 October 2003.

Shelton, Henry. *Joint Tactics, Techniques, and Procedures for Antiterrorism*. Edited by Washington Joint Chiefs of Staff, DC, Ad-A346 716. Washington, DC Joint Chiefs of Staff, Washington, DC, 1998.

Silber, Mitchell D., and Arvin Bhatt. "Radicalization in the West: The Homegrown Threat." edited by NYPD Intelligence Division, 90. New York City, NY: New York Police Department, 2007.

Singer, P. W. "The New Children of Terror." In *The Making of a Terrorist Recruitment, Training, and Root Causes: Volume One: "Recruitment"*, edited by James J. F. Forest, 105-19. Westport, CT: Praeger Security International, 2006.

Stanski, Keith. "Hamas Social Welfare: In the Service of Terror." In *The Making of a Terrorist Recruitment, Training, and Root Causes: Volume One: "Recruitment"*, edited by James J. F. Forest, 136-50. Westport, CT: Praeger Security International, Terrorism, Gender, and Ideology: A Case Study of Women who Join the Revolutionary Armed Forces of Columbi (FARC).

Stemman, Juan Jose Escobar. "Middle East Salafism's Influence and the Radicalization of Muslim Communities in Europe." *The Middle East Review of International Affairs* 10, no. 3 (2006): 9.

Stern, Jessica. "The Protean Enemy." In *Inter/National Security Studies Year 2008 Coursebook*, edited by Sharon McBride, 473-79. Maxwell AFB, AL: Air Command and Staff College, 2003.

———. *Terror in the Name of God Why Religious Militants Kill*. New York, NY: Ecco, 2003.

Tan, Andrew T. H. *The Politics of Terrorism: A Survey*. London, England New York, NY: Routledge, 2006.

Taylor, Peter, and Martin Wilson. *The Third World War, Al Qaeda. America: Hunting for Sleeper Cells*. Princeton, NJ: Films for the Humanities, B. B. C. Learning, British Broadcasting, Corporation, 2005.

The Al-Qaeda Documents: Volume 1. Alexandria, VA: Tempest Publishing, 2002.

Thomas, Mark. "Mark Thomas on Al-Qaeda Recruiting Campaign." *New Statesman* (2003): 13.

Trujillo, Horacio R., and Brian A. Jackson. "Organizational Learning and Terrorist Groups." In *Teaching Terror: Strategic and Tactical Learning in the Terrorist World* edited by James J. F. Forest, 52-68. Lanham, MD: Rowman & Littlefield, 2006.

United States Senate Judiciary Committee on the Judiciary: Subcommittee on Terrorism, Technology, and Homeland Security. *Terrorist Recruitment and Infiltration in the United States: Prisons and Military as an Operational Base* 14 October 2003.

Waller, Michael J. "Prisons as Terrorist Breeding Grounds." In *The Making of a Terrorist Recruitment, Training, and Root Causes: Volume One: "Recruitment"*, edited by James J. F. Forest, 23-40. Westport, CT: Praeger Security International, 2006.

Weimann, Gabriel. "Terrorist Dot Com: Using the Internet for Terrorist Recruitment and Mobilization." In *The Making of a Terrorist Recruitment, Training, and Root Causes: Volume One: "Recruitment"*, edited by James J. F. Forest, 53-65. Westport, CT: Praeger Security International, 2006.

———. "Virtual Training Camps: Terrorists' Use of the Internet." In *Teaching Terror: Strategic and Tactical Learning in the Terrorist World* edited by James J. F. Forest, 110-32. Lanham, MD: Rowman & Littlefield, 2006.

Weinberg, Leonard. "Political and Revolutionary Ideologies." In *The Making of a Terrorist Recruitment, Training, and Root Causes: Volume One: "Recruitment"*, edited by James J. F. Forest, 181-96. Westport, CT: Praeger Security International, 2006.

Wijk, Rob de. "The Limits of Military Power." In *Terrorism and Counterterrorism Understanding the New Security Environment: Readings & Interpretations*, edited by Russell D. Howard and Reid L. Sawyer, 482-94. Guilford, CT: McGraw-Hill Companies, 2002.

Wiktorowicz, Quintan. *The Management of Islamic Activism: Salafis, the Muslim Brotherhood, and State Power in Jordan* Suny Series in Middle East Studies. Albany, NY: State University of New York Press, 2001.

Winnett, Robert, and David Leppard. "Leaked No 10 Dossier Reveals Al-Qaeda's British Recruits." *The Times Online*, 10 July 2005.

Yew, Lee Kuan. "Homegrown Islamic Terrorists." In *Forbes*, 37-37: Forbes Inc., 2005.

Milton Keynes UK
Ingram Content Group UK Ltd.
UKHW030446150224
437844UK00011B/1006